Mastering The Art Of Persuasion:

Strategies for Influencing Others with Integrity and Impact

By Khaled Bouajaja

Content

6. **Ethics and Persuasion:** This axis would explore the ethical considerations that arise when trying to persuade others, including issues of transparency, honesty, and manipulation.

7. **Persuasion in Practice:** This axis would showcase real-world examples of persuasion in action, such as political campaigns, marketing campaigns, and sales pitches.

8. **Overcoming Resistance to Persuasion:** This axis would examine the reasons why people resist persuasion, such as cognitive dissonance and reactance, and offer strategies for overcoming these barriers.

9. **Persuasion in Relationships:** This axis would explore how persuasion operates in personal relationships, including romantic partnerships, friendships, and family dynamics.

10. **Cultural and Contextual Factors in Persuasion:** This axis would examine how persuasion strategies can vary depending on cultural norms, values, and contextual factors such as social, economic, and political climate.

11. **Persuasion and Technology:** This axis would explore the impact of technology on persuasion, including the use of social media, algorithms, and personalized advertising.

12. **Persuasion and Power:** This axis would examine how persuasion can be used as a tool for exerting power, both in individual relationships and in broader societal contexts.

13. **The Future of Persuasion:** This axis would offer insights into the future of persuasion, such as emerging trends, new technologies, and ethical considerations.

14. **Case Studies and Analysis:** This axis would provide detailed case studies and analysis of real-world persuasion situations, examining what worked, what didn't, and why.

15. **Persuasion and Self-Persuasion:** This axis would explore how individuals can use persuasion techniques to persuade themselves, such as changing their own beliefs or behavior.

16. **Mastery of Persuasion:** This axis would offer advice and guidance on how to become a master of persuasion, including ongoing practice and learning, reflection, and feedback.

17. **Persuasion and Leadership:** This axis would examine the connection between persuasion and leadership, and how persuasion skills are essential for effective leadership.

18. **Persuasion in Negotiation:** This axis would explore how persuasion techniques can be used to negotiate effectively, including strategies for reaching mutually beneficial agreements.

19. **Persuasion in Public Speaking:** This axis would focus on how to use persuasion techniques to deliver powerful and effective speeches and presentations.

20. **Persuasion in Sales and Marketing:** This axis would examine how persuasion is used in sales and marketing, including strategies for building relationships with customers and crafting compelling messages.

21. **Persuasion and Change Management:** This axis would explore how persuasion skills can be used to successfully navigate change, whether it be organizational change or personal change.

22. **Persuasion and Decision Making:** This axis would examine how persuasion can impact decision making, both individually and within groups.

23. **Conclusion**

1. Introduction

Persuasion is an art form that has been studied and practiced for centuries. From ancient philosophers like Aristotle to modern-day influencers like Oprah Winfrey, the ability to persuade others has been recognized as a valuable skill throughout human history. Whether it's convincing a colleague to support your idea, persuading a customer to buy your product, or convincing a loved one to see things from your perspective, the ability to influence others is an essential part of our personal and professional lives.

But what exactly is persuasion? At its core, persuasion is the process of convincing someone to change their beliefs, attitudes, or behavior. It's the art of getting others to see things from your point of view, or to take action in a way that benefits both parties. While persuasion is often associated with sales and marketing, it's also an essential part of leadership, negotiation, and personal relationships.

The power of persuasion lies in its ability to inspire action and create change. Whether it's motivating employees to work harder, inspiring a community to come together for a common cause, or convincing a politician to support a particular policy, persuasion has the power to shape our world.

However, persuasion is not without its challenges. Many people are resistant to change and skeptical of new ideas. Others may be more interested in their own self-interest than in the greater good. And in today's fast-paced and information-rich world, it can be difficult to capture people's attention and hold it long enough to make a persuasive case.

That's why mastering the art of persuasion requires both skill and strategy. It's not enough to simply make a compelling argument; you must also understand the psychology of persuasion, the importance of effective communication, and the ethical considerations that come with influencing others. You must be able to anticipate objections, address concerns, and build rapport with your audience.

In this book, we will explore the art of persuasion in-depth, covering everything from the basics of persuasion to advanced strategies for influencing others. We will examine the psychological principles that underlie persuasion, explore the importance of effective communication, and provide practical tips and techniques for improving your ability to persuade others.

Whether you're a salesperson, a leader, or simply someone who wants to improve your ability to influence others, this book will provide you with the knowledge and tools you need to master the art of persuasion. So let's begin our journey and discover the power of persuasion together.

2. Understanding Persuasion:

The hub of understanding persuasion is the foundation of any successful persuasion effort. It involves developing a deep understanding of what persuasion is, why it is important, and the different types of persuasion that exist. By mastering the hub of understanding persuasion, you will be able to create more effective and ethical persuasion messages that resonate with your audience and move them to take action.

At its core, persuasion is the process of influencing others to adopt a particular belief, attitude, or behavior. It is a skill that is essential in a variety of contexts, from marketing and sales to leadership and personal relationships. By understanding the nuances of persuasion, you can become more effective at achieving your goals, whether that means closing a sale, getting a promotion, or convincing a loved one to see things from your perspective.

One of the key elements of the hub of understanding persuasion is the ability to differentiate between persuasion and manipulation. While persuasion is about convincing others to take action based on their own best interests, manipulation involves tricking or deceiving others into doing something that is not in their best interests. By recognizing the difference between the two, you can ensure that your persuasion efforts are always ethical and responsible.

Another important aspect of the hub of understanding persuasion is the ability to tailor your message to your audience. This involves understanding the unique characteristics of your audience, such as their beliefs, values, and motivations, and using that knowledge to create messaging that resonates with them. By doing so, you can increase the likelihood that your audience will be receptive to your message and take action as a result.

Ultimately, the hub of understanding persuasion is about developing a deep knowledge of the principles that underlie effective persuasion. By mastering these principles, you can become a more effective persuader and achieve your goals more quickly and easily.

In addition to understanding the principles of effective persuasion, it is also important to understand the different types of persuasion that exist. For example, persuasive communication involves using verbal and nonverbal cues to influence others, while persuasive writing involves using written language to convince others to take action. Understanding the different types of persuasion and how they work can help you choose the most effective approach for any given situation.

Another important aspect of the hub of understanding persuasion is understanding the psychology of persuasion. This involves understanding the cognitive biases that affect how people perceive and respond to persuasive messages, as well as the emotional factors that can influence their decision-making process. By understanding these psychological factors, you can tailor your message to be more persuasive and increase the likelihood that your audience will take action.

Finally, the hub of understanding persuasion also involves understanding the ethics of persuasion. Persuasion can be a powerful tool, but it can also be used to manipulate and deceive others. As a persuader, it is your responsibility to ensure that your efforts are always ethical and responsible. This means being transparent about your intentions, respecting the autonomy of others, and using persuasion only in ways that benefit everyone involved.

In conclusion, the hub of understanding persuasion is the foundation of any successful persuasion effort. By developing a deep understanding of what persuasion is, why it is important, and the different types of persuasion that exist, you can become a more effective persuader and achieve your goals more easily. Whether you are looking to close a sale, motivate your team, or convince a loved one to see things from your perspective, mastering the hub of understanding persuasion can help you achieve your goals with greater ease and confidence.

To further expand on the hub of understanding persuasion, it is important to note that it is a dynamic process. The principles of effective persuasion are constantly evolving, and new research is emerging all the time. As a persuader, it is important to stay up-to-date with the latest developments in the field, and to be willing to adapt your approach as needed.

One important development in recent years has been the rise of digital media and social networks. These platforms have fundamentally changed the way that people communicate and consume information, and have created new opportunities and challenges for persuaders. To be effective in this new landscape, it is important to understand the unique characteristics of these platforms, and to be able to create persuasive messages that are tailored to the specific constraints and opportunities they present.

Another key aspect of the hub of understanding persuasion is the ability to measure and evaluate the effectiveness of your persuasion efforts. This involves setting clear goals, identifying the key metrics that will be used to measure success, and regularly monitoring and analyzing your results. By doing so, you can identify what is working well, and what needs to be adjusted or improved.

Ultimately, the hub of understanding persuasion is about developing a deep knowledge and appreciation of the art and science of persuasion. It is about being able to create messages that resonate with your audience, using the latest research and techniques to achieve your goals, and always being mindful of the ethical implications of your actions. By mastering the hub of understanding persuasion, you can become a more effective persuader and achieve your goals with greater ease and success.

3. The Psychology of Persuasion:

The psychology of persuasion is a critical aspect of effective persuasion. Understanding the underlying psychological factors that influence how people perceive and respond to persuasive messages can help you craft messages that are more persuasive and increase your chances of achieving your goals.

One important aspect of the psychology of persuasion is the role of cognitive biases. Cognitive biases are mental shortcuts that our brains use to make sense of the world around us. These biases can influence how we perceive information, make decisions, and respond to persuasive messages. For example, confirmation bias can cause us to seek out information that confirms our existing beliefs, while the availability heuristic can cause us to overestimate the importance of information that is easy to recall.

Another important psychological factor that influences persuasion is emotional appeals. Emotions play a powerful role in shaping our thoughts and behaviors, and can be used to create persuasive messages that are more memorable and impactful. For example, using fear appeals can motivate people to take action to avoid a negative outcome, while using positive emotions like joy and excitement can create a sense of enthusiasm and motivation.

Social influence is another important aspect of the psychology of persuasion. We are all influenced by the opinions and actions of others, and social norms play a powerful role in shaping our behavior. Understanding social influence can help you craft messages that are more effective in changing people's behaviors and attitudes.

Finally, it is important to recognize that people are not always rational when it comes to decision-making. Emotions, biases, and other factors can all influence how people make decisions, and it is important to take these factors into account when crafting persuasive messages. This means being mindful of the context in which your message is being received, and tailoring your approach to be as effective as possible.

In conclusion, the psychology of persuasion is a critical aspect of effective persuasion. By understanding the cognitive biases that influence how people perceive information, the role of emotions in shaping behavior, the power of social influence, and the limitations of rational decision-making, you can craft persuasive messages that are more effective and achieve your goals with greater success.

To further expand on the psychology of persuasion, it is important to note that there are different theories and models that can help us understand the psychological factors that influence persuasion. One widely accepted model is the elaboration likelihood model (ELM), which suggests that there are two main routes to persuasion: a central route and a peripheral route.

The central route involves using logical arguments and evidence to persuade someone, and is most effective when people are motivated and able to process information deeply. The peripheral route, on the other hand, involves using cues like celebrity endorsements or emotional appeals to influence people's attitudes, and is more effective when people are less motivated or able to process information deeply.

Another influential theory is social judgment theory, which suggests that persuasion is influenced by the degree to which a message is consistent with a person's existing attitudes and beliefs. According to this theory, people have a range of attitudes on any given issue, and messages that are close to their existing attitudes are more likely to be persuasive than messages that are very different.

Understanding these theories and models can help you craft messages that are more effective at influencing people's attitudes and behaviors. For example, if you are trying to persuade someone to take action on a complex issue, using logical arguments and evidence may be more effective than emotional appeals or celebrity endorsements.

Finally, it is important to recognize that persuasion is a two-way street. In order to be an effective persuader, you need to be able to listen to and understand the perspectives of the people you are trying to persuade. This means being open to feedback, and being willing to adjust your approach based on the reactions and responses of your audience.

In conclusion, the psychology of persuasion is a complex and multifaceted topic. By understanding the different theories and models that underlie effective persuasion, and by being mindful of the attitudes, beliefs, and behaviors of the people you are trying to persuade, you can become a more effective and successful persuader.

4. **The Art of Communication:**

The art of communication is an essential component of effective persuasion. In order to persuade someone, you need to be able to communicate your message in a way that is clear, concise, and compelling. This involves a range of skills, from active listening to the ability to tailor your message to the needs and interests of your audience.

One key aspect of effective communication is active listening. This means being fully present and engaged when someone is speaking to you, and taking the time to understand their perspective and concerns. Active listening involves paying attention to both verbal and nonverbal cues, and responding in a way that shows you have understood what the other person is saying.

Another important aspect of communication is the ability to tailor your message to your audience. This means understanding the needs and interests of the people you are communicating with, and framing your message in a way that is relevant and compelling to them. This may involve using examples and analogies that resonate with your audience, or using language that is accessible and easy to understand.

Nonverbal communication is also an important aspect of effective communication. This includes body language, tone of voice, and facial expressions, all of which can influence how your message is perceived. For example, making eye contact and using a confident tone of voice can help to convey your message with greater authority and conviction.

Finally, it is important to recognize that effective communication is a two-way process. This means being open to feedback and willing to adjust your approach based on the reactions and responses of your audience. It also means being willing to ask questions and seek clarification when necessary, in order to ensure that you are fully understanding and being understood.

In conclusion, the art of communication is an essential component of effective persuasion. By developing your skills in active listening, tailoring your message to your audience, using nonverbal communication effectively, and being open to feedback, you can become a more effective and successful communicator, and ultimately a more successful persuader.

In addition, effective communication requires clarity and brevity. Being able to communicate your message in a clear and concise manner helps to ensure that your audience understands your message and remembers it. This means using simple language, avoiding jargon and technical terms that may be confusing, and being mindful of your audience's level of knowledge and understanding.

Another important aspect of the art of communication is storytelling. Humans are wired to respond to stories, and a well-crafted narrative can be a powerful tool in persuading others. A good story can help to convey complex ideas and emotions, and can help to create an emotional connection between you and your audience.

It is also important to be mindful of the medium through which you are communicating. Different channels of communication require different approaches and strategies. For example, communicating via email requires a different tone and structure than communicating in person or via phone.

Lastly, effective communication requires practice and preparation. Before communicating your message, take the time to prepare and organize your thoughts, and anticipate potential questions or objections from your audience. This will help to ensure that you are able to convey your message effectively and respond to any concerns or objections that may arise.

In conclusion, the art of communication is a crucial component of effective persuasion. By developing your skills in active listening, tailoring your message to your audience, using nonverbal communication effectively, being clear and concise, storytelling, and being mindful of the medium, you can become a more effective and successful communicator, and ultimately a more successful persuader.

One important factor to consider when it comes to the art of communication is the use of emotional appeal. Emotions can be a powerful tool in persuasion, as they can help to create a connection with your audience and evoke a sense of urgency or need. However, it is important to use emotional appeals judiciously and ethically, and to avoid manipulating or exploiting people's emotions for personal gain.

Another key aspect of effective communication is the ability to handle objections and counterarguments. When communicating your message, it is important to anticipate potential objections or concerns that your audience may have, and to be prepared to address them in a constructive and respectful manner. This may involve acknowledging and validating the concerns of your audience, and offering evidence or alternative perspectives to help address their objections.

Lastly, the art of communication is not just about what you say, but how you say it. Your tone of voice, body language, and other nonverbal cues can all influence how your message is received. It is important to be aware of these factors and to use them to your advantage in communicating your message effectively.

In summary, the art of communication is a critical component of effective persuasion. By using active listening, tailoring your message to your audience, using nonverbal communication effectively, being clear and concise, storytelling, emotional appeal, handling objections, and being mindful of your tone and other nonverbal cues, you can become a more effective communicator and ultimately a more successful persuader.

5. Developing Your Persuasion Skills:

The focus of developing your persuasion skills is to become a more effective communicator and influencer. Whether you are trying to sell a product or service, convince others to adopt a certain viewpoint, or persuade someone to take a specific action, developing your persuasion skills can help you to achieve your goals more effectively and efficiently.

One key aspect of developing your persuasion skills is to understand your audience. This involves understanding their needs, motivations, and values, and tailoring your message accordingly. By understanding your audience, you can identify the most effective ways to communicate with them and the types of messages that are most likely to resonate with them.

Another important aspect of developing your persuasion skills is to build trust with your audience. People are more likely to be persuaded by someone they trust and respect, so it is important to establish yourself as a credible and trustworthy source of information. This may involve building a strong personal brand, demonstrating expertise in your field, and being honest and transparent in your communications.

Effective persuasion also requires the ability to anticipate and address objections and counterarguments. By understanding the potential objections and concerns of your audience, you can be better prepared to address them in a constructive and respectful manner, and to provide evidence and alternative perspectives to help overcome these objections.

Developing your persuasion skills also involves being able to adapt to different situations and communication channels. This may involve tailoring your message to different audiences, using different communication styles and strategies, and being able to communicate effectively in different settings, such as in-person, online, or via phone.

Lastly, developing your persuasion skills requires practice and ongoing learning. By seeking out opportunities to practice your skills, such as through role-playing exercises or real-world experiences, and by continuing to learn and improve your communication and persuasion techniques, you can become a more effective and successful persuader over time.

In conclusion, developing your persuasion skills is essential for achieving your goals and becoming a more effective communicator and influencer. By understanding your audience, building trust, addressing objections, adapting to different situations and communication channels, and continuing to practice and learn, you can become a more successful persuader and achieve greater success in your personal and professional life.

To further develop your persuasion skills, it can be helpful to seek out resources and training programs that focus on the art of persuasion. This may include attending workshops or courses, reading books or articles on the topic, or working with a coach or mentor who can provide guidance and feedback on your communication and persuasion skills.

Another effective way to develop your persuasion skills is to seek out opportunities to practice in real-world situations. This may involve volunteering for leadership positions or public speaking opportunities, engaging in debates or discussions with others, or simply practicing your communication skills in everyday interactions with friends, family, and colleagues.

It is also important to stay up-to-date on the latest trends and techniques in the field of persuasion. With the rapid pace of technological innovation and changes in communication channels and social media, it is essential to stay informed and adaptable in order to remain an effective persuader.

Finally, developing your persuasion skills requires a willingness to continually learn and grow. This may involve seeking out feedback from others, analyzing your own communication and persuasion strategies, and being open to new perspectives and ideas. By continually striving to improve your skills and adapt to new challenges and opportunities, you can become a more effective persuader and achieve greater success in all areas of your life.

6. Ethics and Persuasion:

Ethics is an important aspect of persuasion that should always be taken into consideration. While persuasion can be a powerful tool for achieving personal and professional goals, it is important to use it responsibly and ethically.

One of the key ethical considerations in persuasion is the importance of honesty and transparency. It is important to be truthful and upfront with your audience, and to avoid using deceptive or misleading tactics to persuade them. This may involve being honest about your motives and intentions, disclosing any potential conflicts of interest, and avoiding exaggerations or false claims.

Another important ethical consideration in persuasion is respect for the autonomy and free will of others. Persuasion should not be used to manipulate or coerce others into taking actions that are against their will or best interests. It is important to respect the choices and decisions of others, and to avoid using pressure or fear tactics to persuade them.

In addition, it is important to consider the potential consequences and impact of your persuasive actions. Persuasion can have both positive and negative effects, and it is important to weigh the potential benefits and risks of your actions before attempting to persuade others. This may involve considering the long-term implications of your message, as well as any potential unintended consequences.

Finally, it is important to be mindful of the power dynamic between you and your audience. As a persuader, you hold a certain amount of influence and authority over your audience, and it is important to use this power responsibly and ethically. This may involve being aware of your own biases and prejudices, avoiding using your position of authority to intimidate or manipulate others, and respecting the boundaries and rights of your audience.

In conclusion, ethics is a crucial aspect of persuasion that should always be taken into consideration. By being honest and transparent, respecting the autonomy and free will of others, considering the potential consequences and impact of your actions, and being mindful of the power dynamic between you and your audience, you can use persuasion in a responsible and ethical manner to achieve your goals and build positive relationships with others.

Furthermore, ethical persuasion can also have long-lasting benefits. When you use ethical persuasion, you build trust and credibility with your audience. This can lead to stronger relationships, increased loyalty, and a higher likelihood of success in the long term. On the other hand, using unethical persuasion tactics can damage your reputation, erode trust, and ultimately harm your ability to achieve your goals.

It is also worth noting that ethical persuasion is not only important for the persuader, but also for the audience. Persuasion can be a powerful tool for change, and when used ethically, it can help to bring about positive outcomes and improve people's lives. However, when persuasion is used unethically, it can lead to harm, injustice, and inequality.

Ultimately, ethical persuasion requires a commitment to integrity, respect, and responsibility. By adhering to ethical principles and values in your persuasive efforts, you can be a positive force for change and make a meaningful impact in the world around you.

7. **Persuasion in Practice:**

Persuasion is not just a theoretical concept, but a practical skill that can be developed and honed over time. In order to become an effective persuader, it is important to focus on the practical application of persuasion in real-life situations.

One of the key focuses of persuasion in practice is understanding your audience. This involves getting to know the people you are trying to persuade, including their beliefs, values, motivations, and goals. By understanding your audience, you can tailor your persuasive message to resonate with their needs and interests, and increase the likelihood of success.

Another important focus of persuasion in practice is the use of evidence and logic. Persuasion is not just about making emotional appeals or using flashy rhetoric. It also requires a solid foundation of evidence and logical reasoning. By presenting well-researched facts, data, and arguments, you can build a strong case for your message and increase the credibility of your persuasive efforts.

Effective communication is also a crucial focus of persuasion in practice. This involves using clear and concise language, listening actively to your audience, and adapting your communication style to fit the needs of your audience. By communicating effectively, you can increase the persuasiveness of your message and build stronger relationships with your audience.

Finally, perseverance is another key focus of persuasion in practice. Persuasion is not always easy, and it often requires persistence and patience. By staying committed to your message and continuing to engage with your audience over time, you can increase the likelihood of success and achieve your goals.

In conclusion, the focus of persuasion in practice involves understanding your audience, using evidence and logic, effective communication, and perseverance. By focusing on these practical aspects of persuasion, you can become a more effective and influential persuader, and achieve your goals with greater success.

Additionally, it is important to be aware of potential barriers to persuasion in practice, such as resistance, skepticism, and cognitive biases. These barriers can make it more difficult to persuade your audience, but by understanding them and developing strategies to overcome them, you can increase the effectiveness of your persuasive efforts.

Another focus of persuasion in practice is the development of specific techniques and strategies for persuasion. These may include techniques such as storytelling, social proof, scarcity, and authority. By mastering these techniques, you can increase the persuasiveness of your message and achieve your goals more effectively.

Furthermore, it is important to practice and refine your persuasive skills through real-world experiences. This may involve seeking out opportunities to persuade others in your personal or professional life, and actively seeking feedback and self-reflection to improve your skills.

Ultimately, the focus of persuasion in practice is on developing a practical, results-oriented approach to persuasion that can be applied in a variety of situations. By focusing on understanding your audience, using evidence and logic, effective communication, perseverance, overcoming barriers, and developing specific techniques, you can become a more effective and influential persuader, and achieve your goals with greater success.

One important aspect of persuasion in practice is ethical considerations. Persuasion can be a powerful tool for change, but it must be used responsibly and ethically. This means being honest and transparent in your communication, avoiding manipulation or coercion, and respecting the autonomy and dignity of your audience.

Another focus of persuasion in practice is the importance of context. Persuasion can vary greatly depending on the situation, the audience, and the specific goal of the persuasion. Therefore, it is important to be flexible and adaptable in your approach, and to tailor your persuasive message to fit the specific context in which you are operating.

Finally, a key focus of persuasion in practice is the importance of ongoing learning and development. Persuasion is a complex and dynamic field, and new techniques, technologies, and approaches are constantly emerging. By staying up-to-date on the latest developments in the field, and by actively seeking out opportunities to learn and grow, you can continue to improve your persuasive skills and achieve greater success.

In conclusion, the focus of persuasion in practice involves ethical considerations, understanding the importance of context, and ongoing learning and development. By adopting a practical and adaptable approach to persuasion, and by continuously refining your skills, you can become a more effective and influential persuader, and achieve your goals with greater success.

8. Overcoming Resistance to Persuasion:

Overcoming resistance to persuasion is a critical aspect of the art of persuasion. Resistance can take many forms, such as skepticism, disagreement, or outright opposition to your message. However, by understanding the reasons behind resistance and developing effective strategies to overcome it, you can increase the persuasiveness of your message and achieve your goals more effectively.

One effective strategy for overcoming resistance is to focus on building trust with your audience. People are more likely to be persuaded by someone they trust, so establishing a relationship of trust and credibility is crucial to overcoming resistance. This may involve establishing your expertise on the topic, being honest and transparent in your communication, and showing empathy and understanding for your audience's perspective.

Another effective strategy for overcoming resistance is to acknowledge and address potential objections upfront. By anticipating potential objections and addressing them proactively, you can demonstrate your understanding of your audience's concerns and build credibility for your message. This can also help to prevent objections from becoming more entrenched over time, making it easier to persuade your audience.

Using evidence and logic to support your message is also critical in overcoming resistance to persuasion. By presenting clear and compelling evidence to support your argument, you can help to overcome any skepticism or doubts that your audience may have. Additionally, using logical arguments and avoiding logical fallacies can help to build credibility and increase the persuasiveness of your message.

It is also important to understand that not all resistance can be overcome, and sometimes it may be more effective to focus on finding common ground or alternative solutions that are acceptable to both parties. In some cases, attempting to persuade someone who is strongly opposed to your message may only serve to entrench their position further, making it harder to achieve your goals.

Therefore, it is important to be strategic and flexible in your approach to overcoming resistance to persuasion. This may involve adapting your message to suit your audience's values and beliefs, using emotional appeals to connect with your audience on a personal level, or finding common ground or shared interests that can help to build trust and credibility.

Overall, the key to overcoming resistance to persuasion is to be strategic, flexible, and persistent. By understanding the reasons behind resistance, building trust and credibility, addressing objections, using evidence and logic, and remaining patient and persistent, you can increase the persuasiveness of your message and achieve your goals more effectively.

Finally, it is important to remain persistent and patient when overcoming resistance to persuasion. Persuasion is often a gradual and ongoing process, and it may take time and effort to overcome resistance and achieve your goals. By remaining persistent and patient, and by continuing to build trust, address objections, and use evidence and logic to support your message, you can increase the likelihood of success in your persuasive efforts.

In conclusion, overcoming resistance to persuasion is a critical aspect of the art of persuasion. By building trust, addressing objections, using evidence and logic, and remaining persistent and patient, you can increase the persuasiveness of your message and achieve your goals more effectively.

Another important aspect of overcoming resistance to persuasion is to be aware of and manage your own biases and assumptions. We all have our own beliefs, values, and biases that can influence how we perceive and interpret information. It is important to be aware of these biases and assumptions and to actively work to avoid letting them interfere with our ability to communicate effectively with others.

One way to do this is to practice active listening and empathy. By listening attentively to your audience and trying to understand their perspective, you can better anticipate and address their concerns and objections. This can also help to build trust and credibility, as your audience will feel heard and understood.

It is also important to be respectful and open-minded when communicating with others. Avoiding judgment, being willing to consider alternative viewpoints, and acknowledging the validity of others' opinions can help to reduce resistance and create a more productive dialogue.

Finally, it can be helpful to focus on the benefits of your message and how it can help your audience. By emphasizing the positive outcomes that can result from accepting your message, you can help to overcome resistance and increase the persuasiveness of your argument.

In conclusion, overcoming resistance to persuasion is a critical aspect of the art of persuasion. By being strategic, flexible, and persistent, managing your biases and assumptions, practicing active listening and empathy, being respectful and open-minded, and focusing on the benefits of your message, you can increase the persuasiveness of your argument and achieve your goals more effectively.

9. **Persuasion in Relationships:**

The axis of persuasion in relationships focuses on the unique challenges and opportunities that arise when attempting to persuade someone with whom you have a personal or emotional connection. This could include persuading a romantic partner, family member, friend, or colleague.

One of the key considerations when persuading someone in a relationship is the potential impact that your message could have on the relationship itself. For example, if you are attempting to persuade a romantic partner to change their behavior, it is important to consider how your message may be perceived and how it could affect the dynamic between you.

Another important consideration is the level of trust and credibility that exists within the relationship. If your audience does not trust or respect you, it will be much more difficult to persuade them of your message. Therefore, it is important to invest in building and maintaining trust and credibility within the relationship, by being honest, transparent, and consistent in your words and actions.

In addition, emotions can play a powerful role in persuasive communication within relationships. It is important to be aware of your audience's emotional state and to use emotional appeals strategically to connect with them on a personal level. However, it is also important to avoid allowing emotions to cloud your judgment or interfere with your ability to communicate effectively.

Finally, the axis of persuasion in relationships also involves understanding and respecting the autonomy and agency of your audience. While it may be tempting to try to control or manipulate your audience in a personal relationship, this approach is likely to backfire and damage the relationship in the long run. Instead, it is important to respect your audience's right to make their own decisions and to focus on building a constructive and collaborative dialogue.

Overall, the axis of persuasion in relationships requires a delicate balance of emotional intelligence, communication skills, trust and credibility, and respect for autonomy. By understanding these unique challenges and opportunities, and developing the skills and strategies necessary to navigate them effectively, you can increase the persuasiveness of your message and strengthen your relationships in the process.

To further elaborate, persuasion in relationships also requires a deep understanding of the values, beliefs, and needs of your audience. You must be able to listen actively to their concerns, empathize with their perspective, and identify common ground on which to build your argument.

Additionally, the axis of persuasion in relationships involves recognizing and addressing power dynamics that may exist within the relationship. For example, if you are attempting to persuade a boss or supervisor, there may be a power imbalance that affects how your message is received. In such situations, it is important to be respectful and professional, while also standing firm in your convictions and presenting a well-reasoned argument.

Another aspect to consider is the role of communication and conflict resolution skills in maintaining healthy relationships. Persuasion can be a valuable tool in resolving conflicts and finding mutually beneficial solutions, but it must be accompanied by effective communication skills, such as active listening, clear and concise expression of ideas, and the ability to identify and manage emotions.

Finally, the axis of persuasion in relationships also involves understanding the importance of timing and context. Knowing when and how to deliver your message is crucial to its effectiveness. For example, attempting to persuade someone when they are stressed, tired, or distracted may not be the best approach. Similarly, certain topics may be better addressed in private, while others may benefit from a more public forum.

In summary, the axis of persuasion in relationships requires a high degree of emotional intelligence, communication skills, empathy, and respect for the unique dynamics of personal relationships. By developing these skills and approaches, you can increase your ability to persuade those with whom you have a personal or emotional connection, while also strengthening those relationships over time.

10. Cultural and Contextual Factors in Persuasion:

The axis of cultural and contextual factors in persuasion is an important one to consider, as different cultures and contexts may have varying norms and expectations for communication and persuasion. In order to effectively persuade individuals from different cultural backgrounds or in different contexts, it is essential to be aware of and sensitive to these differences.

One key factor to consider is language. Different cultures may have different linguistic nuances and expressions, which can affect how a message is received and interpreted. It is important to be aware of these differences and adapt your language accordingly, while still maintaining clarity and persuasiveness.

Another cultural factor to consider is the importance of social norms and values. What may be considered persuasive in one culture may not be effective in another. For example, in some cultures, direct confrontation and argumentation may be seen as impolite or confrontational, while in others it may be seen as assertive and necessary.

Contextual factors, such as the physical environment or the social situation, can also impact the effectiveness of persuasion. For example, a persuasive message may be more effective when delivered in person, rather than through a written communication. Similarly, certain persuasive tactics may be more effective in a one-on-one setting, while others may be more appropriate in a group setting.

In addition, it is important to consider the influence of broader cultural and societal forces on persuasion. For example, certain cultural values or political ideologies may shape the way individuals view and respond to persuasive messages.

In summary, the axis of cultural and contextual factors in persuasion emphasizes the importance of considering cultural and contextual differences when attempting to persuade others. By being aware of these differences and adapting your persuasive techniques accordingly, you can increase your effectiveness in diverse cultural and contextual settings.

Other factors to consider in the cultural and contextual axis of persuasion include:

- Power dynamics: The power dynamics between the persuader and the persuadee can greatly influence the effectiveness of persuasion. For example, a message may be less effective if it comes from someone with less perceived authority or power.
- Historical and political context: The historical and political context of a particular culture or society can also impact the effectiveness of persuasion. For example, certain political or social movements may be more successful at persuading individuals during times of economic hardship or political instability.
- Social identity: A person's social identity can also impact how they perceive and respond to persuasive messages. For example, individuals may be more likely to be persuaded by someone who shares their same social identity or group membership.
- Communication channels: The communication channels used to deliver a persuasive message can also impact its effectiveness. For example, social media may be more effective in reaching

younger audiences, while traditional media may be more effective in reaching older audiences.

Overall, understanding the cultural and contextual factors that can impact persuasion is essential in developing effective persuasion strategies. By taking these factors into account, persuaders can increase their chances of success in diverse cultural and contextual settings.

11. Persuasion and Technology:

The axis of persuasion and technology is an important aspect of the art of persuasion in today's digital age. Technology has fundamentally changed the way we communicate and consume information, and it has also changed the way we can persuade others.

One important area where technology has impacted persuasion is through the use of social media. Social media platforms provide a powerful tool for spreading persuasive messages, as they allow individuals to easily reach large audiences and to target specific groups or individuals with their messages. However, social media also presents challenges for persuasion, as the sheer volume of information and the ease of sharing means that messages can quickly become diluted or lost in the noise.

Another way that technology has impacted persuasion is through the use of data and analytics. With the rise of big data, persuaders have access to more information than ever before about their target audiences. This data can be used to tailor persuasive messages to specific individuals or groups, making them more effective. However, the use of data and analytics also raises ethical concerns about privacy and manipulation.

Additionally, the rise of new technologies such as virtual reality and artificial intelligence have opened up new possibilities for persuasion. For example, virtual reality can be used to create immersive experiences that can be used to persuade individuals in new and innovative ways. However, these technologies also raise new ethical questions about the use of artificial intelligence in persuasion.

Overall, the axis of persuasion and technology is an important aspect of the art of persuasion, and understanding how technology can be used to persuade others is essential in today's digital age. By leveraging technology in ethical and effective ways, persuaders can increase their chances of success and achieve their desired outcomes.

To be effective in the use of persuasion and technology, it's essential to understand the cultural and contextual factors that shape how technology is used and how individuals respond to it.

For example, different cultures may have different attitudes towards technology and may use different technologies in different ways. Understanding these cultural differences is important when trying to persuade individuals from different cultures.

Contextual factors such as the social, economic, and political climate can also impact the effectiveness of persuasive messages. For example, during times of crisis or uncertainty, individuals may be more susceptible to messages that offer certainty or reassurance. Understanding these contextual factors is essential when developing persuasive messages and strategies.

Moreover, it's important to recognize the potential drawbacks and risks of using technology in persuasion. For example, the use of bots and fake accounts on social media to spread false information can be damaging to the credibility of the persuader and may lead to negative outcomes.

Finally, it's important to recognize that technology is not a substitute for traditional persuasion techniques. While technology can be a powerful tool, it's important to remember that the fundamentals of persuasion, such as understanding the target audience and developing strong arguments, remain unchanged.

In conclusion, the axis of persuasion and technology is an important aspect of the art of persuasion. By understanding how technology can be used to persuade others and the cultural and contextual factors that shape its use, persuaders can become more effective and achieve their desired outcomes.

12. **Persuasion and Power:**

The axis of persuasion and power is a critical aspect of the art of persuasion. Persuasion and power are deeply interconnected, and understanding this relationship is essential for effective persuasion.

Power can take many forms, including social status, wealth, authority, and expertise. Individuals who possess power are often better equipped to persuade others and may have more significant influence over their decisions.

However, the relationship between persuasion and power is complex. Individuals who lack power may use persuasion as a tool to gain power or to challenge existing power structures. Persuasion can also be used to empower marginalized individuals and groups by giving them a voice and influencing the decisions that affect their lives.

The use of power in persuasion can also have ethical implications. Persuasion can be used to manipulate individuals or coerce them into making decisions that are not in their best interests. It's important for persuaders to be aware of their own power and to use it responsibly and ethically.

The axis of persuasion and power also highlights the importance of understanding the power dynamics between the persuader and the target audience. Persuasion may be more challenging when the target audience has more power than the persuader, and it may be necessary to use different tactics and strategies to be effective.

Overall, the axis of persuasion and power is an essential aspect of the art of persuasion. By understanding the relationship between persuasion and power, persuaders can develop more effective strategies and use their power responsibly and ethically.

In addition to the ethical considerations and power dynamics, the axis of persuasion and power also involves understanding how different types of power can influence the persuasion process.

For example, individuals with social power, such as those who hold high-status positions or have large social networks, may be more persuasive simply because of their perceived social influence. This type of power can be leveraged by using social proof or appealing to social norms to influence behavior.

On the other hand, individuals with expert power, such as those who possess specialized knowledge or skills, may be more persuasive when presenting information or making arguments that align with their expertise. This type of power can be leveraged by using evidence-based arguments and providing credible sources to back up claims.

Additionally, individuals with referent power, such as those who are respected or admired by others, may be more persuasive when they appeal to emotions and personal values. This type of power can be leveraged by using storytelling, personal anecdotes, and empathetic language to connect with the audience on a personal level.

Understanding the different types of power and how they can influence persuasion is essential for developing effective persuasion strategies. By being aware of the power dynamics at play, persuaders can tailor their approach to the audience and use the appropriate type of power to be most persuasive.

Another important aspect of the axis of persuasion and power is recognizing the potential for abuse of power in persuasion situations. Persuasion can be used to manipulate or exploit individuals who may be vulnerable or lack power in a given situation.

For example, advertisers may use persuasive techniques to sell products that are harmful or unnecessary to consumers, exploiting their desire to fit in or feel accepted. Politicians may use persuasive techniques to sway public opinion on issues that benefit their own interests, rather than the interests of the public they serve.

In these situations, it is important to consider the ethics of persuasion and to use persuasion techniques in a responsible and respectful manner. This may involve being transparent about one's motives, avoiding manipulation and coercion, and respecting the autonomy and agency of the individuals being persuaded.

Overall, the axis of persuasion and power highlights the complex interplay between persuasion, power dynamics, and ethical considerations. By understanding these factors, persuaders can develop effective and ethical persuasion strategies that benefit both themselves and their audience.

In addition, the axis of persuasion and power also involves understanding how power can affect the reception of persuasive messages. For example, research has shown that individuals who hold more power in a given situation may be less receptive to persuasive messages than those with less power.

This is because individuals with more power may feel less of a need to comply with others' requests or opinions, and may be more likely to assert their own opinions and beliefs. Additionally, individuals with less power may feel more pressure to conform to the opinions and requests of those with more power, even if they disagree.

Understanding these power dynamics can help persuaders tailor their messages and strategies to be more effective in different situations. For example, persuaders may need to use different techniques when trying to persuade someone in a position of power, such as emphasizing the potential benefits and advantages of the proposed action, rather than appealing to their sense of obligation or duty.

Overall, the axis of persuasion and power is an important consideration in any persuasion situation. By understanding power dynamics, persuaders can develop more effective and ethical persuasion strategies that take into account the needs and perspectives of all parties involved.

13. **The Future of Persuasion:**

The future of persuasion is an exciting and constantly evolving area of study. As technology continues to advance, new opportunities for persuasion are emerging, and old techniques may become outdated.

One major trend in the future of persuasion is the use of data and analytics to tailor messages to specific audiences. With the ability to collect and analyze vast amounts of data about individuals' preferences, behaviors, and habits, persuaders can create highly targeted and personalized messages that are more likely to be effective.

Another trend is the increasing importance of ethical considerations in persuasion. As society becomes more aware of the potential for manipulation and coercion, persuaders will need to be more transparent and honest in their messaging. This may involve a greater emphasis on building trust and credibility with audiences, and using persuasion techniques that are grounded in evidence and research.

The role of technology in persuasion is also likely to continue to expand. As virtual and augmented reality technologies become more sophisticated, they may offer new opportunities for immersive and engaging persuasion experiences. Additionally, advances in artificial intelligence and machine learning may enable more sophisticated and personalized persuasion strategies, based on real-time analysis of audience responses.

Finally, the future of persuasion will likely continue to be shaped by cultural and societal changes. As demographics shift and cultural norms evolve, persuaders will need to adapt their strategies to be effective in new contexts. This may involve a greater emphasis on understanding diverse perspectives and tailoring messages to be culturally sensitive and relevant.

Overall, the future of persuasion is an exciting and dynamic field, with new opportunities and challenges emerging all the time. By staying up-to-date on the latest research and trends, persuaders can develop effective and ethical strategies that will be relevant in the years to come.

As technology continues to advance, the future of persuasion will undoubtedly be influenced by the increasing use of artificial intelligence, machine learning, and big data. With these tools, it will be possible to gather vast amounts of data about individuals and use it to craft highly personalized persuasive messages.

However, there are also concerns about the ethical implications of such practices, as well as the potential for manipulation and abuse of power. It will be important to develop ethical guidelines and regulations to ensure that the use of technology in persuasion remains responsible and transparent.

Another trend in the future of persuasion is the growing focus on building trust and authenticity. As consumers become more savvy and skeptical, they will demand more transparency and honesty from those trying to persuade them. This means that persuaders will need to focus on building long-term relationships based on trust and mutual respect, rather than simply trying to sell a product or idea in the short term.

Overall, the future of persuasion will be shaped by a combination of technological advances, changing cultural norms, and evolving ethical standards. Those who are able to navigate these complex dynamics will be well positioned to succeed in the world of persuasion.

Another aspect of the future of persuasion is the increasing use of social media and online platforms for persuasion. With the rise of social media influencers and the ability to target specific demographics through online advertising, there is a growing need for individuals and organizations to develop effective strategies for digital persuasion.

At the same time, there are concerns about the impact of social media on the quality of public discourse and the potential for online echo chambers to reinforce existing beliefs and attitudes. Persuaders will need to be mindful of these dynamics and work to engage with a diverse range of perspectives and opinions.

Finally, the future of persuasion will also be influenced by broader social, economic, and political trends. For example, the growing focus on sustainability and social responsibility may lead to a shift towards more values-based persuasion, while the increasing polarization of political discourse may make it more difficult to persuade individuals with opposing viewpoints.

Overall, the future of persuasion is likely to be shaped by a complex interplay of technological, cultural, and societal factors. Those who are able to understand and adapt to these changes will be well positioned to succeed in the world of persuasion.

14. **Case Studies and Analysis:**

The case studies and analysis hub of a book on the art of persuasion would provide readers with practical examples and in-depth analysis of real-world persuasion scenarios. This hub would showcase a diverse range of case studies from different industries, contexts, and cultures, allowing readers to gain a broad perspective on the art of persuasion.

Each case study would be presented in a clear and concise manner, highlighting the key objectives, strategies, and outcomes of the persuasion effort. The analysis section would then provide a deeper dive into the factors that contributed to the success or failure of the persuasion effort, drawing on relevant theories and concepts from the other axes of the book.

Examples of case studies that could be included in this hub might include:

1. The Pepsi Challenge: In the 1970s, Pepsi launched a campaign called the "Pepsi Challenge," where they set up blind taste tests in public places, pitting Pepsi against their biggest competitor, Coca-Cola. The results

showed that a significant number of people preferred Pepsi over Coke. This campaign helped to increase Pepsi's market share and showed the power of persuasive marketing.

2. Barack Obama's 2008 Presidential Campaign: Barack Obama's campaign team utilized a range of persuasive techniques to engage voters, including emotional appeals, storytelling, and social proof. His "Yes We Can" slogan was particularly effective in creating a sense of unity and hope among supporters, and he successfully mobilized younger voters and minority groups to turn out and vote for him.

3. Apple's "1984" Commercial: In 1984, Apple released a commercial during the Super Bowl that was unlike anything anyone had seen before. It featured a dystopian society, with Big Brother-like figures brainwashing the masses, until a woman carrying a sledgehammer appeared and smashed the screen, representing the arrival of the Macintosh computer. The commercial was a huge success and has since become a classic example of persuasive advertising.

4. The Milgram Experiment: In the 1960s, psychologist Stanley Milgram conducted a series of experiments to investigate the extent

to which people would obey authority figures, even when it meant inflicting harm on others. The results were shocking, with many participants willing to administer electric shocks to strangers when instructed to do so by an authority figure. The experiment highlights the power of social influence and the dangers of blind obedience.

5. The Anti-Smoking Campaign: Over the past few decades, public health campaigns have successfully reduced the number of people who smoke by using a range of persuasive techniques. These include fear appeals, social norms, and appeals to self-efficacy. The anti-smoking campaigns have helped to change attitudes towards smoking and reduce the prevalence of smoking-related illnesses.

Sure, here are a few more case studies:

1. The "Got Milk?" campaign: In the 1990s, the California Milk Processor Board launched the now-famous "Got Milk?" campaign to promote milk consumption. The campaign featured celebrities and athletes with milk mustaches, and the slogan "Got Milk?" became a pop

culture phenomenon. This campaign was successful in persuading consumers to buy more milk and was recognized with numerous advertising awards.

2. The Apple "Think Different" campaign: In 1997, Apple launched a new advertising campaign with the slogan "Think Different." The campaign featured iconic figures such as Albert Einstein, Martin Luther King Jr., and Mahatma Gandhi, along with the Apple logo and the "Think Different" slogan. The campaign was successful in rebranding Apple as a company that valued creativity and innovation, and it helped to revive the company's fortunes.

3. The Dove "Real Beauty" campaign: In 2004, Dove launched its "Real Beauty" campaign, which sought to challenge traditional beauty standards and promote body positivity. The campaign featured women of different ages, races, and body types, and the tagline "Real Beauty" was prominently displayed. The campaign was praised for its message of inclusivity and empowerment, and it helped to boost Dove's sales and reputation.

4. The Bernie Sanders presidential campaign: During the 2016 and 2020 U.S. presidential campaigns, Bernie Sanders used a grassroots

approach to persuade voters to support his progressive platform. Sanders relied on social media and in-person rallies to build a movement around his message of income inequality and universal healthcare. While he ultimately did not win the Democratic nomination, Sanders' campaign was successful in mobilizing young voters and bringing progressive issues to the forefront of the political conversation.

5. The Nike "Just Do It" campaign: In 1988, Nike launched its "Just Do It" campaign, which featured the tagline "Just Do It" alongside images of athletes in action. The campaign was successful in persuading consumers to associate Nike with athleticism and motivation, and it helped to establish the brand as a leader in the sports apparel market. The "Just Do It" slogan has since become one of the most recognizable advertising slogans in the world.

Certainly! Here are some more potential case studies and analyses for the art of persuasion:

1. Political Campaigns: Explore the tactics used by successful political campaigns to persuade

voters. Analyze how the use of emotion, framing, and targeted messaging can sway public opinion.

2. Advertising: Examine the most effective advertising campaigns of recent years, and explore how they used persuasive techniques to sell products or services. Discuss the role of branding, emotional appeal, and celebrity endorsements in modern advertising.

3. Legal Cases: Analyze high-profile legal cases, such as the O.J. Simpson trial, to understand the role of persuasive communication in courtroom proceedings. Discuss how attorneys use persuasive strategies to influence juries and judges, and explore the ethical implications of these tactics.

4. Social Movements: Explore the tactics used by successful social movements to bring about change, such as the Civil Rights Movement, the Women's Suffrage Movement, and the LGBTQ+ rights movement. Analyze how these movements used persuasive communication to gain support, change attitudes, and bring about social change.

5. Business Negotiations: Examine the strategies used in successful business negotiations, such as mergers and acquisitions, contract

negotiations, and sales. Discuss the role of persuasive communication in these negotiations, and analyze how negotiators use persuasion to achieve their goals.

6. Personal Relationships: Discuss the role of persuasion in personal relationships, such as romantic relationships, friendships, and family dynamics. Analyze how effective communication and persuasion can build strong relationships, and explore the ways in which these skills can be developed.

7. Crisis Management: Examine the ways in which companies and organizations use persuasive communication to manage crises, such as product recalls, scandals, and public relations disasters. Analyze how effective crisis management can preserve brand reputation and public trust, and explore the potential consequences of poor communication in these situations.

8. Education: Discuss the ways in which teachers and educators use persuasive communication to motivate and engage students, and analyze the role of persuasion in education policy and reform. Explore the ways in which persuasion can be used to promote lifelong learning and intellectual curiosity.

9. Media and Journalism: Analyze the role of persuasive communication in media and journalism, including news reporting, editorial writing, and public opinion polling. Discuss the ethical considerations of persuasive communication in journalism, and explore the potential impact of biased or misleading reporting on public opinion.

10. Personal Development: Finally, explore the ways in which individuals can develop their own persuasive communication skills to achieve personal and professional success. Discuss the importance of self-awareness, empathy, and active listening in effective communication, and provide practical tips and strategies for developing these skills.

Certainly! In the case studies and analysis hub, readers can explore real-life examples of persuasive situations and analyze them using the concepts and techniques discussed throughout the book. Each case study could include a detailed description of the scenario, the goals of the persuader, the tactics employed, and the outcome of the persuasion attempt.

After reading the case study, readers could be asked to reflect on the situation and analyze the persuasive strategies used. Questions could include:

- What specific techniques did the persuader use to try and influence the other person?
- Did the persuader address the other person's concerns and objections effectively?
- Were there any ethical considerations at play in this situation? If so, what were they and how were they addressed?
- What could the persuader have done differently to improve their chances of success?
- What can we learn from this case study that we can apply to our own lives and situations?

15. Persuasion and Self-Persuasion:

Certainly! Here are some techniques for self-persuasion:

1. Positive self-talk: Use positive affirmations and self-talk to boost your confidence and convince yourself that you can achieve your goals.
2. Visualization: Visualize yourself successfully accomplishing your goals and the benefits that come with it. This can help motivate you and reinforce the belief that you can succeed.
3. Self-reflection: Take time to reflect on your values, beliefs, and goals. This can help you identify any internal conflicts or limiting beliefs that may be hindering your ability to persuade yourself.
4. Cognitive restructuring: Challenge and replace negative thoughts and beliefs with more positive and empowering ones. This can help shift your mindset and increase your motivation to pursue your goals.
5. Goal setting: Set clear and specific goals for yourself and break them down into smaller, manageable steps. This can help you stay

focused and motivated, and track your progress along the way.

6. Accountability: Hold yourself accountable by tracking your progress and sharing your goals with others who can offer support and encouragement.

7. Mindfulness: Practice mindfulness techniques, such as meditation or deep breathing exercises, to reduce stress and increase self-awareness. This can help you better understand your thoughts and feelings, and make more intentional and empowered choices.

As we've discussed, self-persuasion is a powerful tool for personal growth and development. By using techniques such as reframing, visualization, and positive self-talk, individuals can overcome limiting beliefs and achieve their goals. It's important to note that self-persuasion is not a quick fix, and it requires consistent effort and practice. However, the benefits of developing self-persuasion skills are immense, including increased confidence, resilience, and overall well-being. Whether you're looking to make a change in your personal or professional life, incorporating self-persuasion techniques can help you achieve your desired outcomes.

Certainly! Here are some additional points to consider when it comes to self-persuasion techniques:

1. Visualization: One technique for self-persuasion is visualization. This involves mentally picturing yourself achieving a goal or making a change. By seeing yourself in this new light, you can create a positive outlook and increase your motivation to make that change a reality.
2. Positive self-talk: Another technique is positive self-talk. This involves replacing negative self-talk with more positive, affirming statements. For example, instead of saying "I'll never be able to do this," you might say "I can do this if I stay focused and work hard."
3. Rational self-talk: Similar to positive self-talk, rational self-talk involves challenging negative or irrational thoughts with more rational, logical ones. This can help you see things in a more balanced and realistic way, reducing anxiety or self-doubt.
4. Goal-setting: Setting specific, measurable goals for yourself can help you stay focused and motivated. By breaking down a larger goal into smaller, achievable steps, you can build momentum and feel a sense of accomplishment along the way.

5. Seeking support: Finally, seeking support from others can be a powerful tool for self-persuasion. By surrounding yourself with people who believe in you and your goals, you can build a support network that helps you stay accountable and motivated.

16. Mastery of Persuasion:

The axis of persuasion is a multifaceted concept that involves various dimensions, including the psychology of persuasion, the art of communication, ethics, cultural and contextual factors, persuasion and power, and the future of persuasion. Each dimension of persuasion plays a crucial role in our daily lives, from convincing others to support our ideas to being able to persuade ourselves to take action towards achieving our goals.

To become a skilled persuader, one must understand the different techniques and strategies of persuasion, as well as how to effectively communicate with others and overcome resistance to persuasion. Additionally, it is important to be aware of the ethical implications of using persuasion and to consider the cultural and contextual factors that may impact the effectiveness of persuasive communication.

Persuasion is also closely tied to power, as individuals in positions of power often have greater ability to persuade others. Understanding the dynamics of persuasion and power is essential for navigating complex interpersonal and societal relationships.

In the future, the use of technology is likely to play an increasingly important role in persuasion, from social media and online advertising to virtual reality and artificial intelligence. As such, it is crucial to consider the ethical implications of using technology to persuade others and to ensure that the power of persuasion is used responsibly.

Overall, the axis of persuasion offers a comprehensive framework for understanding and utilizing the power of persuasion in various aspects of our lives. By studying and developing our persuasion skills, we can become more effective communicators, achieve our goals, and make a positive impact on the world around us.

The axis of mastery of persuasion refers to the development of one's skills in persuasion to the point where they become an expert in the field. This involves not only understanding the basics of persuasion and applying different techniques, but also being able to adapt to different contexts and audiences, and being aware of the ethical considerations involved.

To achieve mastery of persuasion, one needs to have a deep understanding of the psychology of persuasion, including the different factors that influence people's decision-making processes and the various techniques that can be used to influence them. One should also have a solid grasp of communication skills, including effective listening, questioning, and feedback, which are essential for building rapport and understanding the needs and concerns of others.

Mastery of persuasion also involves being able to navigate power dynamics and overcome resistance, particularly when dealing with individuals or groups who may have different goals or priorities. This requires strong negotiation and conflict resolution skills, as well as an ability to build trust and rapport even in challenging situations.

In addition, an expert in persuasion must be able to adapt to different cultural and contextual factors, as well as new technologies and media channels that can be used to influence others. This requires staying up-to-date with the latest research and trends in persuasion, and being able to apply this knowledge to real-world situations.

Ultimately, mastery of persuasion is not just about convincing others to do what you want, but about building meaningful relationships, creating win-win situations, and fostering positive change. It requires a deep commitment to ethics and a willingness to use persuasion for the greater good.

17.Persuasion and Leadership:

Persuasion and leadership are closely intertwined concepts, as effective leaders often use persuasive techniques to influence their followers and achieve their goals. A leader who is skilled in persuasion can inspire, motivate, and guide others towards a common objective.

One key aspect of persuasion in leadership is the ability to communicate a vision or goal in a way that resonates with others. This involves understanding the needs, desires, and concerns of your audience and framing your message in a way that speaks to them. It also requires being able to articulate the benefits and potential outcomes of pursuing the vision, and to address any objections or challenges that may arise.

Another important aspect of persuasion in leadership is the ability to build trust and credibility with your followers. This involves being transparent and honest in your communications, demonstrating consistency in your actions, and following through on your promises. A leader who is perceived as trustworthy and reliable is more likely to be able to persuade others to follow their lead.

Leaders who are skilled in persuasion are also able to adapt their communication style and approach to different situations and individuals. They are able to read the room, understand the perspectives of their audience, and adjust their message and delivery accordingly. This flexibility and adaptability allows them to connect with a wide range of people and to build strong relationships based on mutual trust and respect.

Finally, effective persuasion in leadership also requires the ability to listen actively and to be open to feedback and different viewpoints. A leader who is willing to listen to and consider the ideas and perspectives of others is more likely to be able to build consensus and to achieve buy-in from their followers. This not only enhances the leader's persuasive power but also contributes to a more collaborative and inclusive organizational culture.

In summary, persuasion is a critical skill for effective leadership, allowing leaders to communicate a vision, build trust and credibility, adapt to different situations, and listen actively to their followers. A mastery of persuasion can enable leaders to inspire and motivate their teams to achieve great things.

Certainly, here are some additional points to consider about persuasion and leadership:

- Persuasion is an essential leadership skill because it allows leaders to communicate their vision and goals effectively and get others on board with their plans.
- Effective persuasion requires that leaders build credibility and trust with their audience. This means being transparent, honest, and consistent in their words and actions.
- Leaders who are skilled in persuasion can inspire and motivate their followers to take action towards achieving shared goals. They can also manage conflicts and negotiate effectively, which are critical skills for leading successful teams and organizations.
- However, leaders must also be mindful of the ethical implications of persuasion. They should avoid manipulating or coercing others and instead focus on building mutually beneficial relationships.
- Finally, persuasion is not a one-time event but an ongoing process. Leaders must continually refine their communication skills and adapt their approach to fit different audiences and situations.

18. Persuasion in Negotiation:

Persuasion is an essential skill in negotiation, as it involves convincing the other party to agree to terms that are favorable to you. In negotiation, persuasion involves presenting your arguments in a convincing and compelling manner, while also understanding and responding to the other party's objections and concerns.

One of the most effective techniques for persuasion in negotiation is to focus on the other party's interests rather than your own. By identifying the other party's needs and motivations, you can present your proposals in a way that meets their needs while also advancing your own goals.

Another important aspect of persuasion in negotiation is understanding the power dynamics at play. Negotiations often involve unequal power dynamics, and the more powerful party may be less receptive to persuasion. In these situations, it is important to find ways to level the playing field, such as by bringing in a neutral third party or by focusing on objective criteria rather than personal relationships.

Active listening is also critical in persuasion during negotiation. By listening carefully to the other party's concerns and objections, you can identify areas of agreement and build trust, which can make it easier to persuade them to agree to your proposals.

Finally, effective persuasion in negotiation requires the ability to adapt and adjust your approach as needed. Different negotiation situations require different strategies, and the most successful negotiators are those who can quickly and effectively adjust their approach based on the specific circumstances at hand.

Certainly! When it comes to persuasion in negotiation, there are a few additional strategies that can be effective:

1. Focus on interests, not positions: Rather than getting bogged down in what each party is demanding or insisting upon, try to uncover the underlying interests that are driving those positions. By identifying shared interests or exploring creative solutions, both parties may be able to come to an agreement that satisfies everyone.

2. Use objective criteria: Similar to the above strategy, using objective criteria can help keep negotiations focused on facts and logic rather than emotions or personal preferences. For example, if negotiating a salary, using industry standards or other objective benchmarks can help both parties come to a reasonable agreement.

3. Framing: How an issue is framed can have a big impact on how negotiators perceive it. By framing an issue in a way that is appealing to the other party or by emphasizing the potential benefits of an agreement, negotiators can increase the likelihood of success.

4. Building rapport: As with many forms of persuasion, building rapport with the other party can be highly effective in negotiation. By establishing a positive relationship, negotiators can foster greater trust, which can lead to more successful outcomes.

5. Knowing when to walk away: While it can be difficult to walk away from a negotiation, sometimes it is the best strategy. If the other party is unwilling to budge or if the negotiation is likely to be harmful in the long run, it may be better to cut losses and move on.

By utilizing these strategies, negotiators can increase their chances of success in reaching an agreement that is satisfactory to all parties involved.

In negotiation, persuasion can be used to influence the other party's perception of the situation, their goals, and their preferred outcomes. This can be achieved through various techniques, such as framing the negotiation in a way that benefits both parties, highlighting common ground, using emotional appeals, and providing evidence to support your arguments. Additionally, active listening and effective communication can help to build rapport and trust, which can make it more likely for the other party to agree to your proposals. Overall, effective persuasion in negotiation involves understanding the other party's perspective, being flexible and creative, and using communication and influence skills to reach a mutually beneficial outcome.

19. Persuasion in Public Speaking:

Public speaking is an art that requires not only effective communication but also persuasion skills. Persuasion in public speaking involves the use of rhetorical devices, storytelling techniques, and other persuasive tactics to influence the audience's attitudes, beliefs, and behaviors.

One of the key components of persuasion in public speaking is understanding the audience. Speakers must know their audience's needs, wants, and interests to tailor their message and approach to better persuade them. It's also important to establish credibility and authority through the use of evidence, statistics, and personal anecdotes.

Another important aspect of persuasion in public speaking is the use of emotional appeals. Emotions can be a powerful tool for persuasion, as they can tap into the audience's fears, hopes, and desires. Effective speakers use storytelling and vivid imagery to evoke strong emotions in their audience and connect with them on a deeper level.

Additionally, repetition, rhythm, and parallelism are some of the rhetorical devices used by speakers to make their message more persuasive and memorable. A well-structured and engaging speech can help the audience remember the speaker's message long after the speech is over.

Overall, persuasion in public speaking requires a combination of effective communication, knowledge of the audience, emotional intelligence, and rhetorical skills. By mastering these skills, speakers can influence their audience's attitudes and behaviors and achieve their desired outcomes.

In addition to the aforementioned techniques, there are some other strategies that public speakers can use to effectively persuade their audience:

1. Establish credibility: Before presenting your argument, establish your credibility as a speaker. Share your credentials, expertise, and experience to give your audience a reason to trust you.
2. Use emotional appeal: Use emotional language and storytelling to create an emotional connection with your audience. This can help to

engage them on a deeper level and make your message more memorable.

3. Use rhetorical devices: Utilize rhetorical devices such as repetition, parallelism, and rhetorical questions to emphasize key points and make your message more persuasive.

4. Use evidence: Use facts, statistics, and examples to back up your arguments and add credibility to your message. Be sure to use reputable sources and present the evidence in a clear and concise manner.

5. Call to action: End your speech with a call to action that motivates your audience to take action based on your message. This can be a powerful way to inspire change and make a difference.

By using these strategies, public speakers can effectively persuade their audience and make a lasting impact.

When it comes to persuasion in public speaking, it's important to understand your audience and tailor your message accordingly. This means doing research on the demographics and values of your audience, as well as their expectations for the event.

Additionally, using rhetorical techniques such as repetition, parallelism, and rhetorical questions can help to reinforce your message and engage your audience. Body language, vocal variety, and storytelling can also be powerful tools for persuasion in public speaking.

It's also important to consider the context and purpose of your speech. Are you trying to inform, persuade, or inspire? Adjusting your tone and approach based on your goals can help to increase the effectiveness of your message.

Finally, being prepared and rehearsing your speech can help to build confidence and ensure that you are able to deliver your message in a clear and convincing manner.

20. Persuasion in Sales and Marketing:

Persuasion plays a crucial role in sales and marketing as it is the foundation of convincing customers to purchase products or services. Successful salespeople and marketers understand how to leverage persuasion to influence their target audience's buying behavior.

One technique commonly used in sales and marketing is the principle of social proof. This principle states that people tend to follow the actions of others in a given situation. Therefore, showcasing customer testimonials or displaying the number of people who have already bought a product can persuade potential customers to make a purchase.

Another technique is the use of scarcity. By creating a sense of urgency, such as limited time offers or limited stock availability, marketers can persuade customers to take action immediately rather than wait and potentially miss out on a good deal.

Persuasion is also used in pricing strategies. For example, anchoring involves setting an initial, high price for a product and then offering a discounted price, making the discounted price seem more reasonable and attractive to customers.

Lastly, marketers and salespeople can also leverage the principle of reciprocity. By offering something of value, such as a free trial or free gift, customers may feel compelled to reciprocate the offer by making a purchase.

Overall, persuasion is a critical component of sales and marketing, and understanding how to effectively use persuasive techniques can significantly impact a company's success in these fields.

Certainly! In sales and marketing, persuasion plays a crucial role in convincing potential customers to buy a product or service. There are several techniques that can be employed to make a successful sale, including:

1. Building rapport: Establishing a connection with the customer is important to gain their trust and understanding of their needs and wants.
2. Understanding the customer's pain points: Understanding the customer's pain points can help identify how the product or service can address their needs.

3. Highlighting the benefits: Focusing on the benefits of the product or service, rather than just the features, can help persuade the customer to make a purchase.

4. Social proof: Providing evidence of the product's effectiveness through customer testimonials or reviews can help build trust and persuade potential customers.

5. Scarcity: Creating a sense of urgency or scarcity, such as limited time offers or limited quantity, can create a fear of missing out and persuade customers to make a purchase.

6. Authority: Highlighting the credibility of the brand or the expertise of the salesperson can help persuade customers to trust the product or service.

7. Framing: Presenting the product or service in a positive light and framing it in a way that resonates with the customer's values or beliefs can increase the likelihood of a sale.

Overall, persuasion in sales and marketing involves understanding the customer's needs and wants, building trust and rapport, and presenting the product or service in a way that resonates with the customer.

Sure, here are some more insights on persuasion in sales and marketing:

1. Focus on benefits, not features: When trying to persuade potential customers, it is important to focus on the benefits of your product or service, rather than just the features. Customers are more likely to be persuaded when they understand how your product or service can help them, solve their problems, or improve their lives.

2. Use social proof: People are more likely to be persuaded by others who are similar to them or have faced similar problems. Use social proof in your marketing efforts, such as customer testimonials or case studies, to show how your product or service has helped others like them.

3. Create a sense of urgency: Persuasion in sales often relies on creating a sense of urgency, such as a limited-time offer or a product that is in high demand. Creating a deadline or scarcity can motivate potential customers to take action and make a purchase.

4. Appeal to emotions: Persuasion in sales and marketing often involves appealing to the emotions of potential customers. Use storytelling, humor, or other emotional triggers

to create a connection with your audience and persuade them to take action.

5. Personalize your approach: Persuasion in sales and marketing can be more effective when you personalize your approach to each individual customer. Use data and analytics to understand their preferences and needs, and tailor your messaging and offers accordingly.

Overall, persuasion in sales and marketing requires a deep understanding of your audience and their needs, as well as a focus on creating a compelling message that resonates with them emotionally and rationally.

21. Persuasion and Change Management:

Managing persuasion and change is an essential skill for anyone in a leadership position, as it involves convincing others to embrace new ideas, methods, or practices. Here are some key strategies to keep in mind:

1. Develop a clear vision: Before you can persuade others to change, you need to have a clear and compelling vision of what that change looks like. This includes both the end goal and the steps required to get there.
2. Communicate effectively: Effective communication is key to managing persuasion and change. You need to be able to articulate your vision in a way that resonates with others and addresses their concerns.
3. Build a coalition: It's easier to persuade others to change when you have a group of supporters who share your vision. Build a coalition of allies who can help you advocate for the change you're proposing.
4. Address resistance: Resistance is a natural part of any change process. Be prepared to address resistance with empathy and understanding,

while also being firm in your conviction that the change is necessary.

5. Celebrate successes: Finally, make sure to celebrate successes along the way. Recognize and reward those who embrace the change, and use their successes to inspire others to follow suit.

6. Clearly communicate the reason for the change: People are more likely to buy into a change if they understand why it's happening. Be transparent about the reasons behind the change, and explain the benefits of the change to the individuals or organization.

7. Address resistance: Change can be difficult, and it's natural for some people to resist it. Identify sources of resistance and address them proactively. Listen to concerns and find ways to alleviate them. Sometimes, addressing resistance might involve finding a compromise or adjusting the plan to better suit the needs of those involved.

8. Involve key stakeholders: Involving key stakeholders can help to generate support and enthusiasm for a change. Identify individuals or groups who will be impacted by the change, and engage them early in the process. This can

help to generate ideas, build support, and reduce resistance.

9. Create a plan and stick to it: Change can be chaotic and uncertain, so having a clear plan is important. Develop a plan that outlines the steps that need to be taken, the timeline, and the individuals responsible for each step. Communicate the plan clearly, and stick to it as closely as possible. Having a plan can help to reduce anxiety and uncertainty, and create a sense of stability.

10. Celebrate successes: Change can be hard work, and it's important to recognize and celebrate successes along the way. Celebrating successes can help to build momentum and create a sense of progress. It can also help to reinforce the benefits of the change and generate enthusiasm for the next steps.

By following these strategies, you can effectively manage persuasion and change, and help your organization thrive in a rapidly changing world.

22. Persuasion and Decision Making:

Persuasion and decision-making go hand in hand. When we make decisions, we often rely on information and opinions from others to help us reach a conclusion. Persuasion can play a critical role in this process, as it can influence the information and opinions we consider and the weight we give them.

One important factor to consider in persuasion and decision-making is the concept of biases. We all have biases, whether conscious or unconscious, that can affect the way we evaluate information and make decisions. For example, confirmation bias is the tendency to seek out information that confirms our existing beliefs and ignore information that contradicts them. This can lead to flawed decision-making if we only consider one side of an argument or ignore important facts.

Another important factor is the role of emotions in decision-making. Emotions can often be a powerful driver of decisions, and persuasive messages that tap into our emotions can be especially effective. However, emotions can also cloud our judgment and lead us to make decisions that are not in our best interest.

Effective persuasion in decision-making involves presenting information in a clear and unbiased way, addressing potential biases, and appealing to both rational and emotional aspects of decision-making. It also involves understanding the decision-making process of the target audience and tailoring persuasive messages accordingly.

Persuasion can also be used to influence the decision-making process itself, such as in the case of influencing the agenda or criteria used in decision-making. This involves understanding the decision-making process and the key decision-makers involved, and strategically framing and presenting information to influence the outcome.

Overall, persuasion and decision-making are closely intertwined, and understanding the role of persuasion in decision-making can help us make more informed and effective decisions.

Persuasion can be a critical factor in decision-making processes, especially in situations where there are multiple options to choose from, and the decision-maker needs to weigh the pros and cons of each option. In such cases, persuasive messages can influence the decision-making process by highlighting certain features of a product or service, emphasizing its benefits over those of its competitors, or even appealing to emotional or psychological factors that are relevant to the decision-maker.

For example, when deciding on which smartphone to purchase, a consumer may consider various factors such as price, brand reputation, technical specifications, and customer reviews. In this scenario, persuasive messages from sales representatives, advertisements, or even friends and family members can play a significant role in influencing the consumer's decision.

Persuasion can also play a role in decision-making within organizations. For instance, a manager may need to persuade her team to adopt a new software tool or implement a new strategy. In this case, the manager may use persuasive messages to communicate the benefits of the proposed change, address potential concerns, and build buy-in from the team.

Overall, persuasion can be a valuable tool in decision-making processes, but it is important to use it ethically and responsibly. Decision-makers should be aware of their own biases and vulnerabilities to persuasion, and should carefully evaluate the information presented to them before making a final decision.

Sure, here are some additional thoughts on persuasion and decision-making:

- Anchoring: This refers to the tendency of people to rely too heavily on the first piece of information they receive when making a decision. For example, if a salesperson starts with a high price point for a product, the customer may be anchored to that number and more likely to accept a higher price than they otherwise would have.
- Confirmation bias: This is the tendency to seek out information that confirms one's preexisting beliefs and ignore information that contradicts them. This can make it difficult to persuade someone who has already made up their mind on a particular issue.
- Framing: The way a message is presented can have a big impact on how people respond to it. For example, framing an issue as a loss rather than a gain can make people more risk-averse and less likely to take action.

- Choice architecture: The way choices are presented can also influence decision-making. For example, presenting options in a certain order or grouping them in a particular way can influence which option people choose.
- Social proof: People often look to others for guidance on how to behave, particularly in uncertain or ambiguous situations. This means that highlighting social proof (e.g. "90% of our customers choose this option") can be an effective way to persuade people.
- Scarcity: People tend to value things more when they are scarce or in limited supply. This can be used to persuade people to take action quickly (e.g. "only a few spots left at this price!").

Overall, understanding the psychology of decision-making can be a powerful tool in persuasion. By understanding the cognitive biases and heuristics that influence how people make decisions, you can craft more effective messages and increase your chances of success.

23. Conclusion

"The Art of Persuasion" is a comprehensive guide to understanding and mastering the various aspects of persuasion. The book covers different techniques, methods, and approaches that are used in various domains of life, including leadership, public speaking, sales, marketing, and negotiation.

The book begins by explaining what persuasion is and why it is an essential skill to have in today's world. It highlights the different types of persuasion and how they are used in everyday life.

The book then delves into the various axes of persuasion, including the axis of power, cultural and contextual factors, technology, and self-persuasion. Each of these axes is explored in detail, providing a deep understanding of how they shape and influence the art of persuasion.

The book includes numerous case studies and analysis to help readers apply the concepts and techniques presented in real-life situations. The analysis hub is a dedicated section that presents various case studies and their analysis to help readers develop a better understanding of persuasion.

The book also covers the mastery of persuasion and how it can be achieved through practice and learning from experience. It highlights the different techniques and approaches used by persuasive leaders to inspire and motivate their teams.

The section on persuasion in negotiation provides readers with a thorough understanding of how persuasion can be used to reach mutually beneficial outcomes in negotiations. It provides valuable insights into the different techniques and approaches used in negotiation and how to apply them effectively.

The section on persuasion in public speaking is a comprehensive guide to developing effective communication skills that can be used to persuade and influence others. It covers the different aspects of public speaking, such as body language, tone, and delivery, that are crucial for effective communication.

The section on persuasion in sales and marketing provides readers with an in-depth understanding of how persuasion can be used to influence consumers' buying decisions. It highlights the different approaches used by marketers to persuade consumers and how to develop persuasive marketing campaigns.

The section on managing persuasion and change provides readers with valuable insights into how persuasion can be used to manage change and bring about positive outcomes. It highlights the different techniques and approaches used to persuade individuals and groups to embrace change and adapt to new situations.

The book concludes with a section on persuasion and decision-making, providing readers with valuable insights into how persuasion can be used to influence and guide decision-making processes.

In conclusion, "The Art of Persuasion" is a comprehensive guide to understanding and mastering the art of persuasion. It provides readers with valuable insights into the different techniques, methods, and approaches used in various domains of life. Whether you are a leader, a public speaker, a marketer, or a negotiator, this book is an invaluable resource that will help you become more effective at persuading and influencing others.

In conclusion, the art of persuasion is a complex and multifaceted concept that is essential in various aspects of life, including leadership, negotiation, public speaking, sales and marketing, and decision-making. It involves the use of various techniques and strategies to influence the attitudes, beliefs, and behaviors of others, as well as oneself. Persuasion is not only about convincing others to agree with our point of view, but it is also about creating long-lasting and meaningful relationships based on trust and mutual respect.

The axis of persuasion provides a useful framework for understanding the different dimensions of persuasion, including the relationship between persuasion and power, the importance of self-persuasion, and the mastery of persuasion. The case studies and analysis hub also provides valuable insights into the practical application of persuasion in various contexts.

While technology is changing the way we communicate and interact with each other, the principles of persuasion remain the same. Therefore, it is crucial to adapt and utilize new technologies to enhance our ability to persuade and influence others effectively.

Ultimately, the art of persuasion is a lifelong process that requires ongoing learning and practice. By mastering the various techniques and strategies of persuasion, we can become more effective communicators, leaders, and decision-makers, leading to greater success in our personal and professional lives.

By understanding the power dynamics at play in persuasion, individuals can develop effective strategies for influencing those around them, whether in leadership, negotiation, public speaking, sales and marketing, or other areas of life. Techniques such as rapport-building, framing, and reframing can be highly effective in building trust and influencing others.

Self-persuasion is also a critical component of mastery, and individuals can develop various techniques to persuade themselves, including visualization, positive self-talk, and goal-setting.

Finally, effective persuasion requires an understanding of the context and the individuals involved. Persuasion in a public speaking context requires a different approach than in a negotiation or sales context, for example. Furthermore, change management is a critical aspect of persuasion, and individuals must be skilled in navigating the resistance to change that often arises in organizations.

Overall, the art of persuasion is a powerful and essential skill for anyone looking to succeed in life, whether personally or professionally. By developing a deep understanding of the various axes of persuasion, mastering self-persuasion techniques, and developing effective strategies for managing change, individuals can become highly skilled persuaders and achieve their goals.

"Readers will find this book on the art of persuasion to be a valuable resource, providing practical insights and techniques to help them effectively influence and persuade others in a variety of contexts."